"In her Blake-vision for the plane
implores and damns. *Ecozoa* is a
plants, rocks and soil, to have th
planet, as the State rides roughsho   ...and
environment. Moore's is an asserti\   ... carth to reclaim
its intactness, its wholeness in the race of human destruction,
human abuse. But it's also calling across time to our human
ancestors, a gathering of the human condition, a roll-call of all
those who have suffered and need to be given voice – accounting for
the costs of human using human for personal and collective gain.
This is nothing less than a declaration of nature's independence,
a manifesto for human engagement that is inclusive, respectful
and aware of the impact all of us make in our day-to-day lives
on the earth's living body. It is passionate and compassionate,
angry but also speaking from within the condition, the crisis.
There's also a vital ecofeminism here that takes responsibility, and
realigns the Goddess as a force for addressing the monopolising
of all religions by the tools of military-industrial violence. And
all of this cased in prophetic utterances underpinned by gritty
realism – blending invocation and reportage. In Moore is a
feminist-Ginsberg-channelling-Blake – a voice we need, a voice
that will not be silenced by vested interests. This is science as
justice, poetry as action. Though deeply crafted, these poems are
no mere ornaments for our consumption. And there's a terrible
beauty in all of this that needs to be understood as an affirmation
of all existence. If the poems hold to account, the book offers us a
means of healing – it is a milestone in the journey of ecopoetics."

John Kinsella
Lauded poet, novelist, critic, essayist, editor
and Fellow of Churchill College, Cambridge

"When your subject is the depredation of the land you must use language as fresh and richly composted as unsullied earth could be. Helen Moore does. She might well be William Blake come back among us, excoriating the wicked and celebrating the body. Her words say the hurts we have inflicted on ourselves because we, and these poems show us this, are of a piece with where we live. I felt colder, warmer, muddier, even the innate unfurling and secure binding of roots, as I read through this unputdownable book. I'm not sure I understood Earth was my planet before I read *Ecozoa*; now I do."

Claire Crowther
poet and critic

"Helen Moore's poetry is the stuff of Deep Time. She speaks the words of our ancestors, whilst dissecting contemporary culture, and has the capacity to hear the voices of the ones yet to come. She is both sage, political commentator and prophet. Helen's language is crafted like the finest sculpture, but this poetry is also visceral and pulsating. She has the ability to stand at the threshold of another world, looking back into this broken time, whilst beckoning us into the promise of the Great Turning. This creates an exquisite tension in her work. This is what poetry should be – beautiful, harrowing, celebratory, passionate, visionary – enabling the reader to experience Life more deeply."

Maddy Harland
editor of *Permaculture* magazine

"'Earth Justice' is an epic masterpiece, a wonderful reincarnation and reinvigoration of the mock ecocide trial."

Michael Mansfield
Queen's Counsel

On *Hedge Fund, And Other Living Margins*
(Shearsman 2012)

"Helen Moore emerges in *Hedge Fund* as an urgent, compelling and compassionate voice for these critical times."

Lindsay Clarke
novelist and poet

"Helen Moore's poems offer a prism to our disquiet about the natural world. Their spectrum encompasses the residual grief of John Clare for the landscape he saw already lost after enclosure, and relishes the hedgerow as an incidentally subversive, liminal space thriving between marked-out areas of greed and ownership. With these poems Moore prods us to our responsibilities, lifts a voice to the act of keeping watch for escalating silences and losses. Her poems are tender, sane, political, born of love, and persuade us that poetry can drive a vital empathy into the fabric of a fragile biosphere."

Sean Borodale
poet and artist

"Helen Moore not only has her own distinctive voice, she has also marked out her own territory, a territory at once local and universal. You could say she has globalised the local or rather localised the global, for her concern is nothing less than our mental and physical sanity, our survival in a dark time. Her poems speak out of the whirlwind, from the depths of her being. They are the laments and keenings of a true makar, speaking to the hearts and minds of those who will listen and then act, before it is too late."

Anthony Rudolf
poet and critic

ECOZOA

HELEN MOORE

Permanent Publications

Published by
Permanent Publications
Hyden House Ltd
The Sustainability Centre
East Meon
Hampshire GU32 1HR
United Kingdom
Tel: 0844 846 846 4824 (local rate UK only)
or   +44 (0)1730 823 311
Fax: 01730 823 322
Email: enquiries@permaculture.co.uk
Web: www.permanentpublications.co.uk

Distributed in the USA by
Chelsea Green Publishing Company, PO Box 428, White River Junction, VT 05001
www.chelseagreen.com

© 2015 Helen Moore
The right of Helen Moore to be identified as the author of this work has been asserted by
her in accordance with the Copyrights, Designs and Patents Act 1988

Designed and typeset by Emma Postill

Cover illustration by Jane Bottomley
Cover design by Tim Harland

Printed in the UK by CPI Antony Rowe, Chippenham, Wiltshire

All paper from FSC certified mixed sources

The Forest Stewardship Council (FSC) is a non-profit
international organisation established to promote the responsible
management of the world's forests. Products carrying the FSC
label are independently certified to assure consumers that they
come from forests that are managed to meet the social, economic
and ecological needs of present and future generations.

British Library Cataloguing-in-Publication Data
A catalogue record for this book is available from the British Library

ISBN 978 1 85623 227 2

ECOZOA

1. THARMAS

Deep Time, Deep Tissue   2

#Iceclimblive   5

apples are not the only gadgets   6

Egford Brook, with Scum   7

The Pocket's Circumference   8

"This is not a dirty protest!"   9

Intimations at Cae Mabon   10

The Ghosts of Fleas   12

I Thank My Ancestors   13

Climate Adaptation, # 1   15

2. URIZEN

Kali Exorcism   18

A History of the British Empire in a Single Object   20

The Flag   23

Cabinet of Curiosities   24

panem et circenses, 44 BCE – 2012 CE   25

Her Feet Speak of the Woman in Heels   26

The Angel of Painting   28

Earth Justice   30

The Ecopsychologist   37

On Sitting for Christopher Twigg   39

3. URTHONA

daughter of dodmen   42

I call on the spirit of Owen   45

Healing Song   46

'The Methodology of the Marvellous'   49

Climate Adaptation, # 2   50

Spaced Out   51

Prayer to the Critically Endangered South China Tyger   53

Succession, Hampton Court Palace   54

Vision, with Product Placement   57

Tetanus Boy, Now! Now!   59

4. LUVAH

Ark Rains, from Aberdeen to Zennor   62

Soul Midwife Sings   63

Sweet Pain   64

'LOVE IS METAPHYSICAL GRAVITY'   66

Aphrodite's Seed   67

glory be to Gaia   68

Our Daily Bread   70

Apple Company, West Country   73

A Natural Curriculum   75

Bio tapestry restored by citizens around the world   77

Notes   78
About the Author   81
Acknowledgements   83

The Ecozoic Era

Ecopoetry is engaged poetry for a new age of awareness, and Helen Moore is a leading light in this probing, ground-breaking genre. Imagine if we were to create a more constructive and hopeful alternative to the human-centred 'Anthropocene', one already named by the great theologian Thomas Berry as the 'Ecozoic Era'. In this approaching time we will live in harmony "with the Earth as our community", in stark contrast to the current period of planetary ecosystems ravaged by industrial civilisation, where apocalypse is widely projected as our collective future, the popular imagination fuelled with sci-fi scenarios of humans abandoning a devastated Earth to colonise outer space.

The word 'ecozoic' has its root in the Greek 'zoe', meaning 'life'. In the complex mythology of William Blake's epic poems *Jerusalem* and *The Four Zoas*, Moore sees the power of the imagination to address the ecological crisis we face. She contemporises Blake's vision, showing how a rebalancing of the 'four zoas' enables us to heal ourselves and our planet, and to establish relationships with self and others that are embodied, heart-connected and able to get to the root of our problems. In this way, fear and limited thinking can fall away, opening up liminal spaces where our love of freedom can flourish and collectively we can sense the evolving futures we most desire. As Berry reminds us, the Ecozoic Era is a phenomenon "we must will into being".

Four Mighty Ones are in every Man; a Perfect Unity
Cannot exist but from the Universal Brotherhood of Eden.

William Blake

… the foundations of a new historical period, the Ecozoic Era,
have been established in every realm of human affairs. The
mythic vision has been set into place. The distorted dream of an
industrial technological paradise is being replaced by the more
viable dream of a mutually enhancing human presence within
an ever-renewing organic-based Earth community. The dream…
becomes the myth that both guides and drives the action.

Thomas Berry

Our task is to take this earth so deeply and wholly into ourselves
that it will resurrect within our being.

Rainer Maria Rilke

It's only a temporary turbulence I'm setting myself against.
I'm in line with the big flow.

Gary Snyder

THARMAS

"Begin with Tharmas, Parent pow'er, dark'ning in the West."

Deep Time, Deep Tissue

For L

Here on the altar to multi-dimensional experience
I'm prostrate and naked (from the waist veiled
with a towel), face ensconced in a leatherette crescent
through which I may disappear

    Your fingers beginning cool, now radiate the Sun
    into layers of dermis, subcutaneous fat
    towards the deeper muscle, at first following the grain
    working with awareness, a mental

    Gray's Anatomy (all red-raw & flayed!) and your honed
    sense of intuition. Slowly, where your deft hands
    press, my body's armour is assuaged – those knots
    tight as rivets, these flat metallic plates

    tensioned as if to snap, these blades tempered
    bands of steel. Time expanding and warmth in oily kneading
    start to release the stress and toxins, which life
    in the Anthropocene engenders in our being

      *

Much later I'll sob like a child
a stream of dammed emotion gushing out
which left me feeling lighter, as if
I really had shouldered a burden

    but for now I float – am foetus
    deep sea mammal
    first bubble of life
    in some primordial lagoon

This aching body that at times
I've hated, softens as its contours roll
this body formed from dust of stars

(ah, the energy rippling through us now!)

Deep time, deep tissue –
eyes form black holes. Sometimes I'm dark matter
drawing everything towards me, swallowing it in
(the way Nut swallows the Sun)
making follicles, cells, poems

This 'me' rapidly collapsing, this 'me'
a mere speck, a gleam in Time's eye
yet developed and refined
over millions of years
in our symbiotic home

    *

Earth, this home that awed
our brave-new astronauts –

    wild, animate planet
    set in cosmic velvet –

inestimable worth, curves
drifting blue and white

    *

O, Anthropocene
period of consequences!

In a pinch of geological time our minds
have made deserts of grasslands

dead-zones in oceans, have cut away
vast sections of rainforest 'lung'

erasing cultures of birds, animals, people
eroding soils elaborated for millennia

We knowing humans
disrupting the grand cycles

of biology, chemistry, geology, knowingly persist
in filling the atmosphere with gases

which trap the Sun's rays
melting glaciers, turning seas acidic

and where our ice-sheets melt
prospect for yet more of Gaia's bitter blood.

O, obscene era
this is an emergency!

*

We breathe, releasing the enormity
of this awareness. How I love

and thank you, dearest Body! You
ancient, four-zoaed temple

open to the skies and aligned to Polaris –
hub around which all other stars

wheel. In whatever mortal span
that remains, help me to navigate

this crisis in our evolution, to stay
with what others have begun

millions of cells rising
in and for our life-source, Earth

willing Ecozoa's birth

#Iceclimblive

After Greenpeace, 11.7.13

You've been going 12 hours (starting 4.20am)
when I find you online –

grainy, flicking pictures like a silent movie, this dizzy
livestream from a helmet-

mounted camera sending intermittent scenes of the Shard's angled
glass, its fakery

of multiple suns and helicopter-wobble in July's heat, while your hands
in black, half-finger gloves

endlessly reaching, this steady belay of ropes to inch you past Shangri-La,
50th floor – and o

my vertigo… the pixel-sized police, ambulance crews, commuters gaping,
pressmen with extended

telephoto-lenses encamped on the pavement, and the glinting tracks of
London Bridge station.

Palms sweating, my heart's under sail towards my larynx as I watch
trending on Twitter

6 women ascending Europe's tallest building (hubristic simulacrum
of our remnant Arctic) –

Viola, Sabine, Victo, Liesbeth, Ali & Sandra calmly enduring
not for the rush

of extreme sport, but as a 'direct communication' with
Royal Dutch Shell (its mute executives

enshrined in nearby headquarters) where it's still
business as usual

apples are not the only gadgets

jaguar is not a big cat of the *Panthera* genus, the threatened
feline of the Americas, but a high-performance engine,
exhaust notes a snarl, an iconic car, *a vision for our future*

apple is not a pomaceous fruit typical of orchards
but a multinational company that designs and markets electronics,
computers, software. (Child labour worsens in its Chinese factories)

winnebago is not the name of a First American tribe
(known also as Ho-Chunk), but a motor home, a lifestyle with compact
coach, rotating 20" TV, vinyl ceiling, and wood effects in mocha cherry

blackberry is not a fruit comprised of drupelets, common
in hedgerows, but a smartphone with apps to change the way
consumers live, work & play. Apparently they *do more – faster*

touareg is not a Berber people, the nomadic pastoralists of the North
African Sahara, but a stylish off-roader – *takes you anywhere you want to go*
(advertising: state-of-the-art hyperbole)

earth is not our wider, life-sustaining body
but a cache of raw matter to be stripped, mined, fracked,
made machines to appropriate the native

Egford Brook, with Scum

For Alex

Heavy rain last night, now the brook runs full
café latte with froth racing downstream

like traffic, the bubbles, but spinning, changing shape
as they go, dirty curdles joining other bits, growing foam;

here & there it hooks itself to branches, rocks –
makes pocked soufflés, milkshake with gunge.

On the bends in the banks, it dumps custard pies,
floats bread & butter pudding by the stones

(where children playing *Squirrel Nutkin*
hopped to Owl Island and got water in their boots).

As if rushing straight from a keg, a head of beer ferments
by a root; midstream, judges' wigs dangle from twigs.

Unsure if all natural organic surfactant,
or discharge, effluent, run-off, detergent

I think, *let the scum rise to the surface, let it be visible –
as without, so within… let's look it fully in the eye.*

Birdsong, sunlight mossing the trees now shedding
their leaves – old things dying for the new.

Sputum, pus, reflux, toilets backing up
party whips, cheesy puffs, media trifles

hurricanes, eddies, undercurrents –
let go the murky stuff… let all the scum pour out!

The Pocket's Circumference

1.

Pale Spock-ear of cotton, a pocket's always turned inwards; and when creased between hip and thigh, is deaf to all but mumbles. A hand's span, with one edge curved, the pocket sinks towards a point, where it gathers dross, broken, dysfunctional items, which rarely represent us; the kind of chaff that congregates out of sight of the general public – like arms dealers, corporate lobbyists & government ministers.

Sometimes, whilst doing laundry, I check a pocket hopefully for banknotes. Invariably empty, but with my hand inside, it soon becomes a puppet. Jawing mutely, it goes through the motions of listening, but in the end ignores me. Often a pocket has already been stitched up.

2.

But here's the rub – don't we all live together in the same pocket? From outer space we see the pale cloud, and here and there the holes. If Earth were a fist balled up and thrust in a pocket, the atmosphere would be as thin as that cotton fabric. Our lungs know this. Drawing 20,000 breaths per day, these twin inflatable pockets point up towards the element on which they depend.

Oxygen dances in from wherever the wind has blown it. Moments ago these atoms stepped out of a leaf. The air we breathe is shared by Doves, Pigs, Cheetahs. Arms dealers, corporate lobbyists & government ministers.

"This is not a dirty protest!"

For Heddar and Alex

It's mud from our boots with which
we smear the cubicles inside the van
where we're detained like grubs
within the pantry cells of larger prey

Three hours without a place to pee
(as in icy rain, friends and comrades wait
to slow the trucks supplying the rig)
whilst we lift the sludge of Barton Moss

with fingertips to daub our prison walls.
*Greater Manchester Police serving crime
fighting Earth's protectors.* On his screen
a cop's observing us – how we form every

letter with the effort of a child. "Filthy
hippies!" On white fibreglass our words
stick. *Fracking poisons earth, water, air.*
We watch our paint dry. The cop thinks

about his overtime, when he'll next see
his kids. Soon he could view us as 'domestic
extremists', if lobbyists hold sway. Mud –
a rich medium in this soiled culture.

Intimations at Cae Mabon

1.

In London, Manchester, Leeds, rain streaks millions of Broad
Countesses and Small Duchesses, cleansing a stone nobility split
and dressed in Wales. But gale-force storms (growing more
frequent) dash them on the terraced streets beneath, and torrential
run-off (increasing in volume) overwhelms the sewers.

2.

Dry, and from certain angles, unworked slate reveals a grain
wrinkled with age, 500 million years – back to when mud congeals
like ashen custard on the Cambrian ocean-bed. Then forcing its
metamorphosis, tectonic pressure begets Snowdonia's ridges,
outcrops, peaks – the highest, Eryri, now resting in a sling of
damp muslin.

3.

Foaming through the wooded valley to the lake, Afon Fachwen
shocks fingers, hand, wrist – wrests the bodymind awake. Dipped
from a pool beside the steps, a fragment in the shape of a chisel
glistens purpley blue through brown. Along each side, its fissile
layers are complex scabs: wound on top of wound.

4.

Mountains mirrored in Llyn Padarn. On a flank of Elidir Fawr,
September splashes Haws, Fly Agaric and Rowan berries amongst
the greys, greens, browns. Here and there stand ruined barracks,
where men from Anglesey would pass the week blasting, heaving,
splitting rock – then Sabbath eve, home in time for Chapel.

5.

Waterfalls, Goddess weeping tears of compassion. Like flaps of
broken skin, Moss peels from stacks of slate. With its thick, damp
pile and woven root-mesh, this is earth skin, a carpet, the trauma

swept invisibly beneath. (Fractured psyche, the armour-plated heart.) All around with slender arms, Birch pluck the stars.

6.

The guttering on the old hospital is red, as if its slates once ran with blood. Above, Dinorwic (world's second largest slate quarry) stares from blank, galleried faces, the mountain's cheeks and nose cut away. And at 2,000 feet, nothing to cushion a fall, no bushes to soften the scree. Just stumps exposed by gunpowder and muscle.

7.

One-time proprietor of Dinorwic, G.W.D. Assheton Smith, Esq., liked hunting, and sailing his yacht. His ancestors acquired much of his 36,000 acreage by enclosing common land, and paying bailiffs to evict the locals from their own ancient quarries. His boast? That the 15 miles from home to Snowdon's summit was every inch his.

8.

Crouched in flannel underwear beside the flickering hearth, a Dinorwic man wheezes, lungs clogged with dust. Hung above the fire, his heavy work-clothes exude a pale fog of steam. Beside him, Elin's caressing the baby. Fists clench. Unbearable her tenderness! Cough. Spit. Swear in English.

9.

Nestled along the icy river, the roofs at Cae Mabon appear as if the land's been lifted – each rustic dwelling raised from under the ground. A youngster leaving care leans against the cob cottage wall, warm sunshine on his face. Descended from a line of damaged men and wives, for the first time he can breathe. Coloured rain-beads drip from the overhanging turf. Alchemy. Last night's ceremony still smoulders in his soul. Rapt attention in the roundhouse: stories, magic, fire. Now he too can begin to wipe the slate clean.

The Ghosts of Fleas

After the painting by William Blake

Ah, the hooked tongues, the bristly thighs,
those simple popping eyes that stare into their bowls,

empty now – no longer will these barber-surgeons
let our blood; instead, rising in their hundreds

from above the house, a flicking, swelling extinction
rite on August's Blue Moon. And still our nerve-ends

jittered, maggot dreams creeping through the curtains –
the unconscious mind knows the prisoner's lice,

the cadaver's wavy flesh. Be gone you
carpet-dwelling fiends; be gone you leaping suckers!

This exorcism by a lethal gas that fogged
the rooms, twisted mouth-parts and innards…

ah, these boards from which they flee;
ah, the stars to which we'll follow.

I Thank My Ancestors

After Joanna Macy

Thank you, infinitesimally Great
Grandmother Worm, for gifting
us the swirl of blood pulsing
through our bodies to feed each tiny cell;

& praise be upon you!

Thank you, Ancestor Fish
for evolving vertebrae that lend our spines
the flexibility to move, to bend,
to walk upon our feet;

& praise be upon you!

Dear Fish, thanks once more
for bequeathing your jawbones
to become the stirrup/anvil/hammer/eardrum
that allow us to hear other beings;

& praise be upon you!

Gratitude, old Cousin Reptile
for a brain that alerts us to danger;
and to you, Paleomammal, for a limbic
system opening us to pleasure;

& praise be upon you both!

Thanks, dear Monkey Sibling,
for developing eyes in the front
of your head. It freed you to climb and leap,
while binocular vision gives us all focal depth;

& praise be upon you too!

To you, Sister Ape, gratitude for sharing
your DNA and your intelligence;
also for hands to learn the use of tools –
may every being pick up appropriate technology!

Then praise be upon us all!

Climate Adaptation, # 1

I'm building ditches, ponds
puddled with clay

I'll grow skeins of Watercress
& webbed feet

my skin may turn subtly
responsive, secrete

moisture like a rounded hymen
my vocal sac

could pulse at mud
the boggy wrack of wetlands

URIZEN

"Am I not God?" said Urizen, "Who is equal to me?"

Kali Exorcism

After Allen Ginsberg

O Kali, shadow-slayer, destroyer of illusion,
I offer up the military-industrial complex,
and all the complexes within me that destroy peace.

Descend, blue-skinned mother, raging, bloodthirsty
fresh from the battlefield of demons, your eight arms
bearing skulls and weapons,

and take this putrid fruit of our violence, slice it
open – to *Ahimsa* expose its seedy flesh
where it will only wither;

then show us the hands of our prime minister and his henchmen
in the pockets of BAE Systems, touting for business
with morbid regimes and crackpot dictators,

and their arms fairs, where they never ask what's fair
in selling arms, just rake in the bloodied money,
as our own banks account to cluster-bomb makers.

Come, dark goddess, tear off veils of rhetoric that conceal
war-mongering deeds in cloaks of respectability; help us
hear deeper than *the pre-emptive strikes, the collateral damage*

ventriloquised by our complicit media,
and demand plain language to describe victims of torture,
rape and murder in the wars they report.

Wild one, let your third eye reflect our distancing tactics –
how we blind ourselves with science, mutely condone prisons
where animals are tested with nerve agents, toxins, explosives.

O Kali, reveal in us all the places where we let the devil make his garden – in scorched earth, leafless forests and among the dumb, black stumps of shattered trees.

O KALI, KALI, KALI, OM, SHANTI, SHANTI!

A History of the British Empire in a Single Object

"The first axiom for camp is… do not make yourself uncomfortable for want of things to which you are accustomed" – Complete Indian Housekeeper and Cook, 1890

I own a Victorian rocking-chair that folds –
a piece of 'campaign furniture'
with which the British Empire was built.
Rockers bear me on a curved sled
mental-travelling across continents,
the seat a plugged lip, which speaks
of indigenous peoples, the hidden values of the antique.
Had I at any moment considered
Mahogany as tree

        a glittering crown which rose above
gargantuan forest skirts? How it began as minute heliotrope
hooked up to the light?
How in dry seasons Mahoganies
would shed their glossy leaves,
baring pugilistic fruit-fists
that were tanned and leathered –
trade winds pummelling out their seeds
spinning them away

to wait for germinating rains?
Nor had my thoughts flown to the Scarlet Macaw
whose crack beak could winkle seeds
from inside those fibrous pericarps;
nor had I walked with tedium-drilled officers
in backabush British Honduras – men who hunted
for sport; who'd have some old Creole bake a pie
with five hundred Parrot tongues.
        In those rainforests,

which the Maya knew as distinctly as kin,
Peccaries wandered, rubbing their scent
against giant buttresses – Mahoganies with girths
wider than the lengths of three prone men.
                                    O, Nine Benevolent Spirits!
O, Maya healers, who observed the Moon's phases;
the motion of bitter sap to trunk or roots;
the absence of dew; and who gathered herbs for teas,
poultices, decoctions. Caoba, Copal, Trumpet Tree,

Sapodilla fruits beloved of Tapir, Paca,
Agouti….   O, brutal British axe!
                    Like convicts at Tyburn, Mahoganies
were quartered, stacked by the tonne for transportation.
Lying below decks, as if so many wounded slaves
piled one above the other, their timbers shifted, creaked,
sap oozing from their fibres.
Then all along the docks, the esteemed furniture-makers
came tapping their canes –

frock-coated men puffed with Honourable
East India Company business,
fingers chiselling at the blood-orange grain,
society minds prizing the exotic wood's
workability, its resistance to decay.
Soon it would be fed to their workers' lathes and planes –
Hillard & Meal, of Craven Street, Strand,
crafting the secrétaires, the sofa-beds,
the travelling rent tables, washstands, chiffoniers

which flaunted comfort and prestige
for Empire's executors.   O, Bengal, Scinde, Lucknow!
                    In this metamorphic chair,
from which a Captain's wife might have come to extol
their crinolined infant, I rock the souls of all those generations
consumed by duty –

Governor-Generals functioning from the collar up;
officers' hearts locked in strong-boxes,
tear-ducts dry as husks;

civil servants melting over pink-tinted maps;
men like living stiffs with swordsticks;
men most at home with mess silver and big-game trophies;
men who had no intimate equals –
womenfolk pecking, preening their clipped wings,
and their mute, invisible offspring.
O, white folk with your self-invoked burden
of superiority –
all this furniture of an expanding state.

The Flag

April 23rd, St. George's Day

How proudly they've hoisted it
above the greening valley!

From that glossy pole it flutters
limply, a butcher's bandage

shorn from the cloth of Albion.
This to fete the slain Dragon?

I would rather keen its death,
mourn the sainted mission

that yields the calamity
of Earth's energies oppressed,

ancient vision twisted
into man versus beast.

Ah, and what an abject maypole!
No kith or kin to interplay

their ribbons – instead, a trembling
head, its cross a fragment of the web

which our early ancestors
tracked across these isles.

And that cross is their line in us –
a resurrection in the fecund season

when blood ripples
on England's winding sheet.

Cabinet of Curiosities

For Adam Horovitz

Exhibit A

Moral compass, 21st century, made in Taiwan. Set in black plastic casing with a bevelled edge, the silvered hand defaults to West, and has been engraved – the craftsman's arm braced, heart-rate slowed to make each minute stroke exact. Magnified, the words read: "You are, therefore I profit."

Exhibit B

High horse, old grey nag, not what she used to be, stands one hand tall. Provenance: indignation, outrage at all species of hypocrisy, injustice, lies, double-dealing, at which she grows twenty times her usual size – bucks all trends. Status: put out to grass, but making a come-back. Not yet extinct.

Exhibit C

Pearl of wisdom, 4mm diameter, opaque like rice milk, but weirdly gleaming. Date: timeless. Provenance: China, rare – believed stolen from among a Dragon's leathery jowls. Bequeathed by the poet-thief, she writes of the experience: "I obliged myself to face the all-consuming monster."

panem et circenses, 44 BCE – 2012 CE

With Christopher Lloyd, from What On Earth Happened?

Imperial propaganda & entertainment	*24/7CNNFoxSchnewsreality*
as a means of popular control	*HollywoodMcOlympicsIpad3*
were Roman innovations	*bungabungaSuperMarioMTV*
which substantially reduced	*BigSkyBrotherRupertTeaParty*
the risk of internal unrest	*HarrywarslikeplayingXboxWii*
in an empire short on expansion	*celebritiesTwitterRoyalJubilee*
but addicted to growth	*NASDAQFTSE100GDP*

Her Feet Speak of the Woman in Heels

"This little piggy went to market..."

You'd think a walking head
which we ferry here & there –
this upright, overactive biped
in & out of boardrooms, shops,

evening dos in blahniks/choos,
heel-bones dying on those plastic stalks
that flourish arse & calves & boobs
like ornamental plants,

but make of us disfigured cranks
with hammer-toes & devil's claws.
Slipshod, & not a word of thanks
for fifty years of constant work –

how many more pricks
of conscience does a person need?
Corns, bunions, blisters –
foot-soldiers of somatic wars,

these wounds on which she shambles,
& we, bald poultry
squeezed in tiny sandals
cry out, *we're really free-range*

digits – & long to rootle
unimpeded, browse though dewy
meadow grass, wander footloose
until sundown....

At dawn, we'd rise mercurially
from dreams, shake ankle-wings
for ancient tarsal memories,
phalanges which recall

chopines, clogs, poulaines;
& more blissful eras when
nakedly we kissed the streets –
once, when heads had feet!

The Angel of Painting

December 2011

And she appears like this epiphany in a small Galician bar
on the Portobello Road. Diminutive, with tufted russet
hair, creaturely, her eyes set in charcoal shadows

around the upper sockets. Human, yes, radiant
and somehow ageless, as if dropping in from eternity –
sonorous Paula, all of Lisboa floating about her.

She smiles at me, and I find I'm looking at her soul
as she grins there beside me
gazing in at mine.

*

O, and I was heavy with the company
of unreconstructed men! Drawn into their orbit,
I'd been so patient as they exercised their egos –

subtle forms of control, lesser
& greater put-downs, the talking space
commandeered. Too patient,

too English, for several days I bore
their fuddled thought & fear
like a silly martyr.

*

Do you sweat when you make poems?
There she is grinning again, and for a moment
I've no idea how to answer.

My poems come from dreams, sometimes from meditation,
I reply, ignoring the grind, the push, the stickiness in my pits –
all the labour to be rid of a hectoring inner critic.

*

Her Christmas card commissioned by Dulwich Picture Gallery
is the Virgin giving birth. In a white cotton nightie, she reclines between thighs
of a swan-winged midwife, who wears the scarlet underskirts

and jaded features of a 'slut'. Wickedly Paula smiles,
describes the fizz that angelic finger made
when inserted in Mary's aching cunt.

*

How to dine beside these Regos?
There were tapas, *champiñones al alioli*
washed down with cava and fino.

Mostly I tasted the upward rush of coming to –
of being in this presence
that made me virgin in my power.

Earth Justice

"I don't want to frighten you, but not a stitch can be taken
On your quilt unless you study. The geese will tell you –
A lot of crying goes on before dawn comes." – Robert Bly

For Polly Higgins

1.
What reason might I have to fly
with unknown Waterbirds to Canada?
(Reason which is not derived

from corrosive profit
or the scientific abstract.)
Oil, synthetic crude

which brokers world warming, hunger, war,
and ecocide, the international crime;
ecocide, destruction of life.

> …] At the Supreme Court, London, September 30th, 2011,
> Michael Mansfield for the prosecution, unwigged
> and in black European silks, resembles a learned Silverback:
>
> *the reason that I'm mentioning this*
> *is that it's the first time an offence*
> *has been tried under the act …*
>
> In the dock stand the CEOs of Global Petroleum
> and Glamis Corporation –
> Clerk of the court: *Mr Bannerman, Mr Tench,*
>
> *you are here today on the following indictment:*
> *as a consequence of extracting Tar Sands*
> *in Canada, the peaceful enjoyment*

by the inhabitants of that territory
has been severely diminished,
thereby putting birds at risk of injury and death,

contrary to sections 1 and 2 of the Ecocide Act 2010.
Mr Bannerman and Mr Tench, how do you plead?
The defendants: *Not guilty.*

To their left Mansfield QC represents the absent victims –
Canvasback; Goldeneye; Canada Goose; Lesser Scaup; Mallard
killed by toxic sludge:

a mix of bitumen, polycyclic hydrocarbons, acids, sand, clay
which coats feet, legs, feathers, makes tarred anchors
of these sitting Fowl – drags them down with lazy bubbles

to bite the dregs of our addiction.
Oil, that ancient sunlight. That liquid gold
which fuels our fast-lane rage,

commuter lifestyles,
convenience meals….
"O, for a cut-price bottle of Californian red!"

(Middle Britain's choice,
tranquilising,
TV pig-out.)

…] There are agreed facts in this case,
but 'extensive' is clearly
a term of art, not science…

Which bulletin showed exactly how their wings were glued?
One Spring, so many boomerangs of birds
migrating up the Mississippi flyway,

pursuing the great river system –
those long syringes of light,
shafts, filaments

carrying them North… North to Athabasca, from where
they'd never return. It takes so many kilojoules of energy
to lift-off when burdened…

> …] the principle of strict liability,
> mens rea does not apply here –
> as they said at the Nuremberg trials,
>
> individual responsibility is important,
> you can't hide
> behind a fiction.

Having travelled thousands of miles
each Bird was primed for Summer on the marshes,
the deep teal lakes fringed by Spruce, Jack Pine and Tamarack –

those light, buoyant months to court, or pre-paired, to mate….
Along the way there'd been breaks, bills scooping up clear water,
preening, wing-shaking, delicious spray on plumage,

a dabble down for something
succulent – at each dive
the ripples spreading wide.

Then on hollow wing-bones, a first eye-view, a fragment
of Boreal forest – yet more hectares gone –
and vast gouges in the ground,

a gigantic bite, teeth-marks as long as streets,
the 'overburden' dug away to leave a gangrened mouth,
open pits the size of Boston, D.C., Chicago,

> …] Bearing in mind the Boreal forest
> has taken since the Ice Age
> to get to the state it's now in… 10,000 years, 5,000 years…

You'd have thought the successive skeins of Canvasback, Goldeneye,
Canada Goose, Lesser Scaup, Mallard
might have noticed the strange brown water, the rainbow slicks?

How long for tired Ducks to learn new tricks?
　　　…] This 'processed water,'
　　　hypoxic zone,

which swallowed them like men dressed in lead.
And o, how the bitumen burned
their throats, their internal organs –

　　　…] we're dealing with vast areas here,
　　　These are lakes,
　　　Not ponds.

2. Pondlife

… recall your worst case of heartburn, and multiply
by ten thousand. This is caustic soda passing through your gut. Excretion
is impossible. One hour later, you're dead.

　　　…] Mr Tench: These things are unavoidable
　　　if we are to continue the essential
　　　employ of oil to the Western world."

3.

petroleum you're ubiquitous I do not love you stink
petroleum I rinse you from my follicles my scalp
petroleum you're inside my mouth get out
petroleum you press against my thighs do not
petroleum inside my cunt your manufactured lubricant
petroleum fuck you stop pushing yourself on me
petroleum doesn't hear is just dead animals plants
petroleum a second skin I wish I could go naked
petroleum slips down my oesophagus lurks in my rectum
petroleum slides in through my anus watch how I explode
petroleum sick bastard I'm drowning in all your useless tat
petroleum I've had enough you leave me no choice goodbye
petroleum is that you still following me
petroleum you may be silent but I see your dirty prints

4.

Question: what is most costly
and yet impossible to cost,
and so to some seems worthless?

> ...] Mr. Mansfield: *An ecosystem is termed*
> *as a biological community of interdependent living*
> *organisms and their physical environment*

Echo palace of the hyperboreal
formed through random acts and synchrony –
a mutual call and response that lifts sap-filled columns,

spires, vaulted ceilings, halls with fleeting mirrored floors
etched with branches, and in fine weather, frescoed clouds, sky –
this place that holds open windows,

restores draperies in every shade of green;
makes wind-sculpted pulpits for Herons,
brackish sacristies for Insects, Amphibians;

is an ancient tapestry, which changes daily,
and though exquisitely conserved,
supports the Dene to hunt and fish;

is an ephemeral gallery,
where webs are hung with moonstones,
and trawling white hulls, Swans court their own reflections....

> ...] Mr Tench: *We were and are licensed*
> *by the government,*
> *as in every other country where we operate,*

Here symmetries are made, and broken,
become patterns of form – concentric circles
where Ducks dive – patterns of sound –

...] there's a pattern we weren't able
to predict –
the birds arrived prematurely

a Mallard scorning its wake;
and each day, the improvised arrangements
of this Boreal orchestra:

Aspens trembling with the rasps of Shrike
and Warblers' high incisions;
reedy whistles of White-throated Sparrows

in the tops of Birch,
while from a wind-ruffled lake, the Loons' mournful wailing
all make each moment

a concerted movement,
each sound unfurling
from its niche...

Answer: these desolate wastes
pitied by the Christian mission;
these godless crusts awaiting our consumption.

5.

...] Mr Bannerman: there's nothing
that can be humanly done
to prevent a bird landing in a lake or pond.

...] Christopher Parker QC: this case of Robin
Bannerman, scapegoat extraordinaire

6.

Ah, and what justice for beloved ones
who sing and speak in other tongues?

7.

...] Judge Norman: *Members of the jury,*
you are the sovereign judges
of the agreed facts in this case

...] *causing injury to 2086 birds,*
causing death to 2303...

...] *When you determine whether ecocide is established*
you have regard to tests of size,
duration and impact

...] *Canada is a highly industrialised nation,*
a member of the Commonwealth...
the fourth richest economy in the world.

...] *It is not a defence to say*
operations were licensed according to national rules
and were operated in accordance with the terms

...] *has the question of leakage from the ponds*
into the ground water, the Athabasca River
ever come up at board level?

...] *Members of the jury,*
it's now time for you to consider.

8.

...] Judge Norman: *I think we have a verdict.*
Shall we call them in?

The Ecopsychologist

In memoriam Theodore Roszak, 1933 - 2011

"When in obedience to a narrow reality principle, we make the non-human world less than it is, we also make ourselves less than we are. More of the mind is split off and driven into that zone of impermissible experience called 'insane'." – Roszak

With the ecozoic hands of a new Renaissance man
who knelt in floor-to-ceiling temples of visionary books,
complex forests, flew to eyries, strode with magma for legs,
you reached into my head, parting waves
of left and right brain – and there, in the rocky depths
put your finger on the primal umbilicus –
that psychic cord which links me to my alma mater, Earth.

For centuries I'd been taught to shovel shit
against this holy portal – spade after spade,
information hoarded for the sake of information,
piles of disenchantment that built a vast dam,
a numb wall on the topography
of my inner world. And how impregnable this citadel
of single vision, thought reduced to boxes, compartments.

Divided from myself – and from the source
of energy that keeps the soul vital, rooted in its wider body –
I felt grey, weak, desperate.
But your mental medicine became a hurricane
blowing in my mind, and your words sparked a green fire,
stoked a wild desire to tear down the edifices
junking my horizon.

At times nightmares came seething through cracks,
but I'd learned to see them all

as facets of collective dreaming – to thirst
for drops of this oneiric fluid in which the ego swims.

Clear streams now pour over the rubble,
and I taste an intelligence held across millennia –
how to be human in nature.

On Sitting for Christopher Twigg

It's how he sees me, or doesn't, that he's working,
barefoot in long grass,

and I'm on the patio, immobile in his mother's faded chair,
and he's looking

impassive like a Chinese sage, but in a grey felt fedora,
the charcoal poised beside

the thick, receptive paper he's clipped and taped onto an easel,
while I gaze beyond –

beyond and through the tuning fork of Apple tree into thickets
of subtly moving foliage –

and then he begins, striking the paper, drumming, raining
marks in chance patterns,

chaos impressed on paper – Christopher's sense of atoms
dancing where I am;

and then he stops, steps back, waves his arms as if to help
him take off,

and returns to rubbing out, to inscribing new marks
while I, outwardly still,

lower myself into an artesian well of being, breathing;
hear the Blackbird's *will, will,*

see him flying back and forth like Christopher's charcoal –
a model of patience and persistence,

the low parabolas he describes across the garden
in search of Insects, Worms –

a nest amidst the Honeysuckle's pink fingers fanning
out against the fence;

here at the top of the slope, which sweeps down to the stream,
I'm aware

of the infinite curve of the Earth's surface, of pricking Midges,
mewling Buzzards;

of the Sun appearing through clouds, and of I shuttering my eyes,
lids like wooden slats;

of leaves moving in and out of focus, and of how I'm quietly
part of this –

and that this me, whom Christopher sees, is moving between,
is pouring through the gaps;

I, who's swallowing, blinking in his mother's faded chair
is a trick of light;

how versions of me which surface, and are momentarily caught,
may be ancestors, aspects;

that there are moments when I feel infinitely sad, wise;
times when I see

faces nodding through trees – how I too may rise up
and become a foliate head.

URTHONA

"I was Urthona, keeper of the gates of heaven."

daughter of dodmen

Avebury, c. 2700 BCE

child of the stones, i sparked here on may morning
in a bed of wild garlic, was born beside an eel pool
at oimelc, when udder-milks flow, birch saps rise.

now fifteen years on, i return
through women's mysteries and menses, chosen
as handmaid *to she who sees.*

of the honour i needn't speak –
enough just to be here in the sanctuary,
which is the serpent-dragon's head, around us the mottled veils
of darkness as we wait for dawn's creep.

with spirals of deep-red ochre my body
has been daubed by the women pressing quietly at my back;
besides this, i wear deerskin, bead-bones,
and for strength these boar-tusk totems.

> *blessings on bone hag*
> *who hides in the barrows*
> *when the earth gets the horn –*
> *her shadow never leaves!*

daughter of dodmen – lineage of geomancers
whose dowsing staffs alighted
where the giant stones would come to stand –
i bow my head, fear's torc pressing cold and hard around my belly.

why should i quiver when i've washed at the wellspring,
circled it nines, and chanted our songs?
with my kin i've honoured the greenwoods –

haunts of deer, ox, boar to whose spirits we've prayed,
thanked for gifts of blood, meat, bone.
afterwards we fired up our beacons on the roundy hills,
and gladdened at the sight of other fires distantly beyond;

then, driven between the flames, our herds
were cleansed, now chew dreamily in meadows
jewelled with cuckoo flower, cowslips and day's eyes.

o, that i were still cradled by my kin
who stand invisibly above the all-swallowing ditch! dug by my forebears
with antler picks and ox-bone shovels, this mighty earthwork
radiates the power of our open-air temple.

courage, child, and patience! for some time the tribes
have up held their palms to the stars, attuned to moon-with-child
and to the web of sacred sites and track-ways crissycross these lands.

a night without sleep and with much merriment
yet still we stand; our stones charged by the union
of sun, moon and vortices of water will raise those who lay
hands on their cool, craggy surface.

i mustn't fear *bone hag* – i'm grown up and charmed
from the doings of mischief. yet even *she who sees*
trembles like a reed, sensing for the moment
to begin…

soon i'll lend her my sapling frame and crooky arm –
i, elder-bridge, she, in hide cloak and horns
decked all feathery and blossom, moving like drunk,
the bristle-thin flint drowsing between those bulbous, wrinkled breasts.

slowly we'll pass together through the body of serpent –
an avenue of two hundred paired stones glistening like teeth in this heavy dew.
then, at the gateway to the outer circle, i'll wait steadfast –
let the ringing stones wash through me.

from the first inner circle – the solar eye
that lies beside the lunar – we'll scan the eastern hills
to watch sun limning up. as its ruby charge touches our eyes,
the earthen banks will rock with drumming, roaring, clapping,

and the energy will swell, grow enormous –
white lights may even dance amongst the stones, bending stalks
of grasses, tracing cups, rings, spirals.

dragon energy awoken – beneath our naked feet we'll feel it,
springs seeping out to wet the banks of this temple womb.
then, as sun climbs higher in the sky, it will heat the cock-stone,
its long shadow licking at the gapey-hole of cunt-stone beyond.

> blessings on bone hag
> who hides in the barrows
> when the earth gets the horn –
> her shadow never leaves!

at last the *cunctipotent* one will throw back her cloak,
and arms splayed like wings, she'll rise into the air, hovering above
like a hawk spying out its prey.

now her thunderous voice will roll around the hills,
and her utterances will foretell summer's harvest,
the boons, woes and ills of our people.

when it's done i'll lay myself – shoulders, hip and thigh one with
all-mother, sweat gleaming on my neck, where the bristle-thin flint
will draw a new string of beads… bright thanksgivings
to bless hallowed ground.

and must keep open my eyes
fixed on bear
who guides
                    each spirit home

I call on the spirit of Owen

Gas! Gas! Quick boys!

Ah, Wilfred, how your cries resound in my head
but parroted by corporate vampires & undead
politicos all eager to suck, to pound
the last molecules of gas from deep underground.

Among all those poor lads' bones
Wilfred, you knew *the tale of leaves,*
of smothered ferns set down in prehistoric stone –
and so assist us now to keep the gas within its shale
that it may never flare/escape/incinerate.

(And may the frackers' drills go soft, their stocks & shares evaporate!)

Still, witness the new lies peddled by fossilised minds
with licences, with mineral bribes
Funds! Funds for the boys! – the entitlement of State.

Healing Song

I non-brand unbranded woman
no logos   no ticks on me   they fall through the holes says
we permeable membrane woman
feeling this life-blood thinned with poison
heart haemorrhaged on her cotton sleeve
soul rising up through cracks
Plantain pushing through tarmac
Self-heal   insurgent mauve in lawns
she being powerful and mysterious says
with Maria with Anne we find the ancient tracks
we listening-ear woman   collective ear to ground
of inner/outer wildness   a know-it-all/know-nothing woman
divided self   she who would be whole

born with Sun in Taurus
bull-amongst-china   child of matter/Mater
divided from   our greater body/Mother
a not-good-enough/good-for-nothing woman
beautiful child bewitched with lies
this system making self-hating/-hurting woman
wailing sibyl   a broken addicted woman
woman divided   trying-to-be-whole

a go-crazy vertiginous woman
red rag to inner coterie   victim whore self-saboteur
from the cocoon/state of limbo   I let go I let go
white Western woman   her father's daughter
authoritarian father/rebel child   connected to him in spirit
she who howled at his passing and sang his spirit home
(borrowing text from *The Tibetan Book of the Dead*

because she didn't know how else)
she who's one with her ancestors   she who sometimes forgets
we divided   trying to be whole

she a neglected vine
shrivelled grapes leaves stems
tendrils curling out through mortar, panes
we scattered in our power
we atoms blasted in seas of original Chaos
she bearing traces of Sabre-toothed Tiger Mayfly Sloth
slave empress witch   gasping in millpond
'I' whose atoms are in you now
she sinking in a vat of carcinogenic soup
says we think/look/feel   better on clean food
ape-woman munching Hairy Bittercress
aching for human-Earth community
divided   longing to be whole

she drowning in information says
the world's burning up   there's little I can do
we must begin right away   we
night woman/day woman   cells infused with pneuma
we shadow woman   watching my shadow
hands making sacrificial Hare   woman who sacrificed her hair
took scissors   cut off long silky chunks
she aching for lineage   to cunning-folk knowledge
she trusting it's still encoded in us now
I peeling myselves like onions
crisp outer skin   the raw inner layers
that often make her weep   she fist-waving
hurt woman divided   trying to become whole

mother-to-my-inner-child woman
who delights in laughter   who longs for your arms
woman with balls penis breasts cunt   alchemical hermaphrodite
soul descending   to meet her demons

toasts them with eau-de-vie   hopes/trusts
she'll trail a golden string back out
we of dark/of light   yin   yang woman
she perceiving light only from darkness   says
MOTHER   MOTHER   MOTHER
why do we kick beat   rape   your precious body?
divided   we who would be whole

woman of Sun Moon planets stars
winding the ball   spiral-time being
born with silver-plated spoon says
we unbranded   escaping the giant slave-ship market
tattooed as rite of passage
we who enter dream-time   who learn to trust our dreams
spin from the World Tree
she you I   root-&-branch woman says
'she' who never will be   whole
in healing ourselves we begin to heal   the whole

'The Methodology of the Marvellous'

After Gloria Feman Orenstein

"The marvellous is the eruption of contradiction within the real".
– Louis Aragon

Surefooted in her shoes of raw gooseflesh
my guide bears a light, leads me off the edges
of maps, along the famine lanes and coffin routes

of the uncanny. Gap-toothed she smiles,
cackles at recurrences, opens doors to messengers,
points silently at omens. All around, tsunami-scale seas

swallow people down – data sucks away
their souls, dumps them in monolithic quangos,
wrecks them up on watersheds, at cross-roads.

Questing for the perennial, I chance on books,
find anamnesis hived within their covers –
sense how it eases me within.

When I move with awareness, my guide is always there
to prompt me – turning a corner I see
how a word reflowers in another seeker's mouth.

Climate Adaptation, # 2

The Sun presses down with many hands –
we are pig iron smelted in the furnace; Trafalgar
Square bakes like Tahrir Square without its people.
And we have slowly adapted – come out at night
when it's cooler, stroll the canals fashioned
by the uprisings of the Thames. Little Venice
has spread; we're the Venice of the North
now the original has gone. And there's no choice
but to be in what's left of Europe – Mother
Earth has moored humanity together at her table,
and she's at the centre of all our decisions.
From our boat, I watch the river swimming
with the gibbous Moon; we use her light to sow
our seeds, and harvest every month when she dies.
We live by lunulations – have become silvery,
left-handed humans, who see their shadows;
and feminine in ways that men and women
had forgotten how to be. My Beloved & I
have taken rooms in a Moon Palace – we enjoy
the circularity of life inside the straw-bale towers
with our fine lunar gardens out on the roof. At dusk
the neighbourhood collective meets to plan
the night's work. The scent of Jasmine
sweetens the air; in the dark I've heightened senses
for finding all our herbs & medicines.
Like our planet, we're slowly convalescing.
To celebrate, my guild of astronomers has polished
Aluna – our tidal-powered Moon clock may be copied
by surviving cities all around the world.

Spaced Out

It was a close-run thing   wasn't it?
I mean, watching you   a century from now

     ensouled, emplaced, engaged

in outloving/outwitting the colonists   (spiritual warrior)
their limitless horizons   expanding   in all directions
claiming space   towers & spires
needling   the clouds
uprooting humans forests, animals, plants
the wild preserved in nominal enclosures

     Cuckoo Lane, Primrose Hill

their fantasy inventing ever new   frontiers
till Gaia had been girdled   with this homogenous project

     ('scientific materialism')

And   in   their   privileging of Reason
they'd become so un-reasonable   that for a while
we disembodied beings

     (awaiting our next incarnation)

feared our projected future –   spaced out
         like prisoners   inside blank-eyed pods & capsules
floating colonies of limbs   amputated from home

     no Lilac-scent, no birdsong, no salt-rush of ocean

And o, how we willed you, early 21st century humans
to draw on your courage, your wildest hopes & visions
your faith in the ultimate blessings of service   to withstand
their torture, their desecration!

Did you sense how sometimes we'd lean in, rebalance
your feet, or that we'd speak... (those rare, but shattering
voices)?

How we'd lead you to open that email/weblink
at that synchronous moment

how we'd cross your path with silvery insistence
pointing the way?

Of course you laboured mostly in the dark
but occasionally you'd see the Moon eclipse
a skyscraper glinting beside it

Sometimes you felt so small, so a t o m i s e d
your mind encased in iron – no, you couldn't possibly secure
humanity's survival   alone!

But already millions were rising right around the globe
and linking up you led each other
towards a distant speck of light – that portal through which
thanking you – our wise, brave ancestors – with shrieks & wails
we'd enter the world   would grow

One century on   we thrive in woody folds
flowering fields and Gorse-clad dunes.
          Look, our forests have been replanted and the seas
                              are gradually receding....

Prayer to the Critically Endangered South China Tyger

Soul-dweller of forests,
bequeath us your mystery – all intuitions that creep,
stealthy dreams and hunches

that seize us out of nowhere,
bearing us in burning jaws through the hidden jungle.
And let us keep our questions –

if – like us – you were random chance,
or born from the furnace
of some divine brain?

Either way, let these thoughts bring awe;
wake us from endless sedation by data,
from the drab empires

of all we lose touch.
Seemingly invincible, in our cities of fiction,
we've scorned the flaming pelt

you wrapped around our hearts,
have doused the embers in our bellies
where wildness used to lurk;

for we'd wish no one, no thing
to prove us vulnerable – and ignore the broken
lines of your shadow.

All this you'll take as you pass, Tyger,
finally from Earth – but grant us the fierce desire
to hunt a bright vision for tomorrow….

Ah! And teach us how to rewild ourselves!

Succession, Hampton Court Palace

A gobby phantom in the Great House of Easement,
Harry slaps the thighs of courtiers
who once fawned beside him (doublets & hose
mounded at their feet), boasts of Stags he's hunted in the park;
or how he spanked his mistress
behind the Hornbeam hedges of 'The Wilderness'.

Absentmindedly a gardener's winding his watch
forward & back – he'd like to see the Great Vine,
feel its grapes coming fat as plums;
but the Chief Conservator's decreed
maintenance today, and so the gardener checks –
yes, that Hedera is next: "Remove for conservation of the royal ironwork."

A plant with the powers of Hephaestus,
for years the Ivy's gripped these square bars,
which teams of blacksmiths forged to keep the rabble out –
tentacles thickening, slowly constricting,
at will she bends the *great spykes of irne*
as if white-hot from the hearth.

Come on, start! The gardener with face buried
in his hat's latticed shade, stoops to draw his tool into
petrol-hungry life. At its snarl, the Ivy's fate
looks set – trunk & branches must surrender
their petalled shales of rust.

But aren't her emerald pennants still flicking in the wind –
a sign she'll succeed every king & queen?
And today, perhaps her time has come –
that long imagined future when the chainsaw dies
in the man's hands, and at Harry's former seat,
wilderness is finally revived?

*

54

Inside the palace, front-of-house is down
and costumed guides at ticket-booths
droop like courtiers in *The Tale of Sleeping Beauty*;
the Orangery's visitors stare – forkfuls of cake frozen mid-air;
only Kathryn Howard
stirs in the galleries and cloisters.

Now the restoration can properly begin –
in cavernous kitchens Rats demolish
mocked-up Tudor dishes,
then ransack feather-beds for their nests;
in the Privy Garden, dead heads wither on stems;
parterres are besieged by weeds;
and the Great Vine cracks through panes,

its fruit the prize of Starlings.
Days, weeks, months pass – storms blow windows in;
Tapestry and Carpet Moths feast on antique weaves;
Hedgehogs nest in drifts of unswept leaves
while Fallow Deer graze the topiary
restyling all the Yews into punks and other fiends.

In the Great Hall Death-watch Beetle
burrows in the marrow of the hammer-beam ceiling,
ticking like bombs. Clouds twist about the red-brick chimneys,
spill their load – gargoyles no longer spout
and water seeps within, without.

Damp grows happy & glorious –
in State Apartments it warps the muralled gods,
bedevils Gibbons' sweetest cherubs,
incites plaster to collapse onto four-poster beds.

As centuries of grace & favour glide away,
a colony of Bats has come home to roost;
from the Chapel Royal's *paynted timbers*

they hang like gnostic gospels on the lips of beggars –
a high kind of treason
as Great Harry turns in his grave.

Vision, with Product Placement

Night-time on a medieval street, a place where ghosts and angels mingle. Here a shaven-headed Hare Krishna in orange robes sets up a stall. Soon sweet chilli is exuding from his metal pot. Tenderly he pours a cup for all who come – the drunken, the broken-hearted, the down-and-outs, the Muslims, Jews, Pagans, Gnostics, Hindus, Sikhs and capitalist insomniacs.

Sipping YOGI TEA ®, their fragile egos soften. A man looks into another's eyes, sees fear masking a profound desire for love. They talk on, laugh, cry, hug. Others do the same. Suddenly all judgement, all tribalism is gone. Here's tea serving humanity!

And yet the darkness continues – inside the giant cage, sirens wail, people howl, pass out on the couch, 24/7 headlines flashing from their screens. But as the Sun gilds the dirty streets and unloved gardens, there's a buzz that isn't breaking news.

Where once billboards peddled fantasies of happiness, whitewash obliterates it all. Now every hoarding proclaims a different message.

Love is letting go of fear. Passers-by start; spontaneous exchanges break out between strangers. Children smile and old men cry for the second time in their lives. *Without you the Universe is not beautiful.* A woman with a hare-lip becomes a believer.

Stuck in traffic, commuters frown. *Fast running doesn't guarantee meeting a destination.* Stepping from sleek cars towards a lobby of developers, three borough councillors flush at the omniscience: *You are not for sale!*

The Sun continues to shine. *May your mind learn to love with compassion.* Police cars race up and down, lines of enquiry are pursued. Mid-afternoon, minions are sent to remove this anti-consumerist propaganda. But people protest, knock down their ladders, plead that it stays.

A muttering tramp squints from the shadows. Where just last night he dozed beneath the polished smile of business, he now considers how: *Our thoughts are forming the world.*

Tetanus Boy, Now! Now!

After the Scraptor sculpture by Paul Boswell and Rachel Macleay

1.

Do not weep, George Stubbs –
this stocky boy built from scrap
stands proud nonetheless.

Do not rue his shoddy gaskin
or fetlock, the pox of mattress springs
oxidized on neck and flanks;

nor mind his fistulous withers
underwired with cables
stripped of their copper;

in fact this barrel-body houses all
his vital parts – a vacuum-cleaner hose
functions well as windpipe,

a greasy chain as vertebrae,
while a motor and its coiled tubes
serve for heart and guts.

Clearly he's not a fine beast –
but this is *art brut*, an equine creation
outsiders will doubtless admire.

2.

Redeemed for draught-work,
he clatters down the lane
his heavy body hauling felled Pines;

he's even sought after as a stud
now that forests have been divided
into five-acre holdings.

Once dark and oppressive, these plantations
are cut for timber-framed dwellings,
fuel to burn, sell or barter,

and the land is used for growing food.
Our countryside supports mosaics
of coppice, smithies, mills,

and our towns and cities are fringed
with allotments, orchards, farms.
Now nothing goes to waste –

and in these transitioning times
the Horse resumes
ancient sovereign power.

LUVAH

"I see not Luvah as of old, I only see his feet
Like pillars of fire travelling thro' darkness & non entity."

Ark Rains, from Aberdeen to Zennor

For N

To work her sympathetic magic
Noah's girl has pilfered from every last
haberdashers, and drops her haul, pounds
of pins & needles stabbing at the tarmac –
aquapuncture making waves across our streets.
Suddenly the sea arises where it never did before,
and gone that old-style British drizzle – now a month's
precipitation tips down in a day, secret archives
are unleashed, a family's silver squirreled
under a bathtub: candlesticks, napkin rings,
tureens, ladles, platters, canteens of bright
cutlery rattling down the roads – and factories
springing up to churn out more, mass markets
swelling rivers within minutes, huge aching sheets
that crumble our defences, break into homes, leave
insurers wringing out their hands, packing sandbags,
heading for the hills in a loss adjustment of mud, as anchor-
men & women stoically report yet another freakish storm –
a one in one hundred chance.

                              *

Ah, sighs Noah's daughter, *these rains*
are all the tears that people never shed,
but the drops bouncing from their noses
will help them to open up their ducts.
At this, she smiles, unbuttoning
her beloved as they shake themselves free
from their clothes. Naked and beautiful,
they writhe, couple. *Deep water!* she whispers.
Arching, they become a pair
of Great Whales conjoined, diving
to the ocean bed.

Soul Midwife Sings

Bush Wren, come to my left breast
where no child sucks –
let me cup your spirit in my hands, feel
its weightlessness, a ticklish essence.

In your tiny beak you held
so many threads, and now they fray,
are severed. I bless you for your gentle
featheriness plucked from the tapestry

we struggle to preserve.
Grand Cayman Thrush, here too
let me cradle you as if your tremulous
wing were broken –

but your name is just an echo,
a hidden spirit of the place where money
laughs, does all the talking.
Come, come Flame Brocade Moth,

Pyrenean Ibex, Javanese Lapwing,
Red-bellied Gracile Mouse Opossum,
Bory's White Bat, Bachman's Warbler,
Silver Trout, Passenger Pigeon –

my arms are nearly wide enough
to nurse all this grief at your passing.

Sweet Pain

For Tess

Before I bled this month, my breasts ached so much
it felt like they'd amassed half the world's
suffering. My homeopath said it's progesterone –

a sign of ovulation, and I think, *Christ,*
how did I get this old and not know?
because, some months now, they just don't,

and today, for the first time in my life, it hurts
that I'm not going to have a child.
Of course, I'd surrendered to my doubts –

the fear I'd go mad, follow Sexton, Plath,
because it takes a village to raise a child
and I never had that.

Besides I own various thorns and inner
hooks – my child would have been obstinate,
rebelling as much as I did – and I couldn't

watch myself snag him/her in anger, break
that bud of youth. So I've chosen to embrace
different responsibilities – to journey through

my wounds to serve The Great Turning.
Now let revolutionary love suckle
at my breast – the desire's been growing

for some time, and I've brought my watering-
can to seeds of loving kindness;
watched my prickly jealousies

crimson-petalled judgements and intolerance
wither within. Sometimes it's such graft
I wish I'd grown from other rootstock –

yet I know my strengths arise from struggle.
Holy child, drink my resource!
I'll walk from these tears a fraction taller.

'LOVE IS METAPHYSICAL GRAVITY'

Down the side of the hairdresser's, this e-generation
graffito – spontaneous scrawl of exuberance,

new consciousness indigo child/late
love-child of baby boomers, a rebel angel,

free thinker who's done drugs to peel
layers of conditioning from his/her mind;

also a free lover in the sense of life's erotic
potential, the faith in love as the highest force

for good – not just (or even) God,
but the divine in all of us; our profound capacity

for redemption because there's no such thing
as evil – only love-starved people.

And how healing, the trance-dance
DJ pumps it up in biochemical hearts,

to the beat, waves of hands, wrists, arms –
a submarine world, its flowing bodies

like Eelgrass in underwater light,
a world where everyone is love, learning

to open, move in the mutual attraction
of other beings… like Earth, Moon, Sun –

love on a high, yet this culture grounded in
and nourished by the ecstatic.

Aphrodite's Seed

Cool to her initial touch, a golden
sphere concealed within her palm
emanates the clear scent
of Autumn mornings, when
old Spider Woman weaves

her orb between the jagged arms
of a Rosebush. The kitchen knife
descends through skin
& watery flesh – now laid apart,
both hemispheres reveal

the pentacle of Venus. Fruit
of her rose-line encirclement of Gaia,
five coarse pouches and in each
the shiny, brown tips
of Aphrodite's seed.

glory be to Gaia

glory be to Gaia,
for rainbows, glaciers and fresh snow;
we honour & praise you, Gaia,
mysterious blue planet
unique in this vast universe;
like your widest rivers our hearts
flow with gratitude.

glory be to Gaia,
for forests, valleys and exquisite flowers;
we honour & praise you, Gaia,
great mother,
thank you for clean air and water,
and all the fruits and seeds
manifest through your abundant power.

glory be to Gaia,
for birdsong, mountains and clear lakes;
we honour & praise you, Gaia,
giant pulsating orb of life
from which we've grown –
please help us feel our interdependence
with all animal and human kin.

glory be to Gaia,
for millipedes, worms and all tiny creatures;
we honour & praise you, Gaia,
ceaseless wheel of life,
we embrace your eternal cycle,
the rich soil our bodies will become,
and the gift this present moment is.

glory be to Gaia,
for whales, phosphorescence and fish;
we honour & praise you, Gaia,
planet-jewel of the cosmos,
sacred being infused in our dna;
please light the spark of peace in us
that we may serve this precious life.

Our Daily Bread

On the restoration of Talgarth Mill, Black Mountains, 2011

Seed   crust   dense body   crumb –

    at lunar Lammas here on Mynydd Du
        giving thanks for water, fire, steel,
where reclusive springs rise,
    begin their descent;

atoms of hydrogen clasped by two of oxygen
        tumble through Cwm Dwr-y-Coed
            (Valley of Water & Wood),
                land of shorn Ewes, who browse behind the shelter
    that Bracken fronds provide;

above, slate-grey cumulonimbus
        (streaked as if the Sun just raked out its embers)
sees itself as liquid plying glassy lips of stone,
    dark hairy mosses,
        falling strands of come;

swift flight of rotting debris, bark, leaf,
        a sheep-skull nodding like the Moon;
here we sit to cleanse our minds,
    make empty kists of bone –
        back-to-back our bodies form
          a Janus box
            sounding upstream & down;

    in-breath, hum circling
        round wind-torqued Hawthorns – Birds drawn
          to the hearth of our chant;

and on past stands of late Foxglove
    the pagan-hooded stems that worship the Sun,

epiphanies that fall through chasms in the cloud,
the solar equanimity in blessing all the brooks
which now make common cause

before   precipice pours
into ancient woodland,
& trees cling to gulleys scoured by its path;

here in Cwm Pwll-y-Wrach, torrents –
pressure-wash on mud-stones
carving beds, tables, steps,
dumping Stork-nests of wreckage;

but downstream, how the river shrinks,
spreads a laundry of silks
where Dippers come to peck;
marbles enigmatic patterns – water-light on trunks;
hush, as the air shimmers with Coal Tits' piercing *tisou-tisous*;

then through a tunnel-shade of Hazels
spitting nuts in its pools,
it tinkers down the valley
refreshing the roots of Meadowsweet
as it serpents into town;

there, tripping over boulders, it falls again, again,
smoothes itself back out,
kneads the feet of stone houses,
bubbles by the lovers huddled on a bridge –
flirts with us, makes postcards,
recalls how it's changed
course,

is autonomous
yet willing to slip back in harness,
replenish the headrace
(old familiar, a pleasant sensation)

lend its resource as onto the wheel the Ennig roars,
     fills the oaken buckets
     (slotted hands sparkling as the mighty wheel tips),

          rumbles the axles,
               & deep within the mill,

               these massive shafts which drive the spinning grin –
                    cogs, teeth
               that turn the granite stone

               where grist, rushing through its eye,
         is crushed   feathered into sacks:

         baker   dough   town fired up.

Apple Company, West Country

On a crisp day when we gather
round our trees in boots, scarves, woollens,
they can seem so closed and sparse –
just the Lichen and the Mistletoe
dressing the January bark. The Wassail Queen
shivers in her cloak and thin-soled pumps,
and a boy dreams aloud of hotdogs;
but the sharing of our cup
mulls our thoughts, starts the circle.

Industrial apples have
some of the highest pesticide
residues of the world's most
commonly consumed fruit.

Expectations go sky-high
with May's cumulus of blossom. We head out
again to breathe the warming air;
listen to the Song Thrush,
the rumours of Bees;
how the Cuckoo echoes our longing
for the world to grow and fruit.

Many foreign producers
spray up to twenty times
in a growing season –
a practice that yields more

Rain falls in August.
Our orchard drips on glistening skins,
on Wasp beneath a leaf umbrella.
Inside, kids watch TV, or read
between the lines. Now we dream of

"perfect" looking apples.
Most supermarkets prefer this
to the blemishes so common
on home-grown produce.

Apple Day,

when neighbours wheel in barrow-loads
of Russets, Bramleys, Beauty of Bath,
and our year draws its circle.
We savour pies and spiced cider,
while older children roost in trees above
toddlers playing 'Pin the Maggot'.
Then the Blood Moon waxes on our feast,
and dusk draws each family home,
a new belonging in this company of apples.

A Natural Curriculum

"Let Nature be your teacher." – William Wordsworth

I am child-free, but have a dozen children
who come to me for help, comfort –

a soft-skinned hand in mine, unshaped
by experience, yet eager to feel, to learn;

that three-hundred-year-old Beech standing taller
than a church – what history has it witnessed?

Holding a lens, a child sees
the slant, black eyes and furry legs

of a Honeybee, whose waggle-dance
we've been learning to mimic.

Released from the boxed-in logic of classrooms
we open to the gifts and surprises

of landscape, seasons, weather – wild November gusts
that send us wheeling like Buzzards;

fruiting-bodies wearing butter-yellow caps
and us, dentist-like with mirrors, inspecting gills

white as teeth; or we find a fleshy Earthworm
probing leaf-litter like a peeled finger – Worm, our top

recycler, who teaches zero waste in Nature.
Outdoors, we encounter words, patterns, numbers,

infinite lessons in care, symbiosis.
Hedges constitute our school, each wood

a state-of-the-earth project – that fallen trunk
the perfect beam for learning balance.

With twigs we build skeletons
as anatomically correct as each maker's age

or interest can manage. Older children become bigger
brothers, sisters – together we form a tribe

skilled at foraging, fire-craft, cooking up stories.
Leadership comes in praise, listening,

boundaries. Amidst these saplings I too am learning
to grow towards the light

Bio tapestry restored by citizens around the world

"The blue and the dim and the dark cloths/Of night and light and the half-light…"

earthguardian.org, Sunday 10 February 2013 7.20 GMT

> ***One of the supreme achievements of the known Universe***

a stitch lost here & there
a species, a loch, a forest
for decades it had been falling
into states of disrepair

> ***its survival over billions of years is little short of miraculous***

with parts *déjà* destroyed
by the construction of armadas
& thousands of armies slashing
its fibres, missiles deployed

> ***the exceptional size & complexity, the harmony & freshness***

its strands ceaselessly torn
by industrial fishing & farming
endless consumption leaving
our embroidered toile so worn

> ***of its colours, of its artistry, & the genius of its guiding***

that in some places where
lives vanish through holes
people see how *futu* the future
& begin mending the tears

> ***spirit combine to make it infinitely numinous***

Notes

Deep Time, Deep Tissue

The current geological epoch, named the Holocene, encompasses the growth and impacts of industrial civilisation on our planetary ecosystems. Given these impacts, which have global significance for the future evolution of all living species, a new term 'Anthropocene' was proposed in 2000 by Paul Crutzen & Eugene Stoermer to denote the present time interval. However, critics say that this overstates and reinforces a human-centred perspective, and deprives us of an inspiring vision for a new ecological age.

In the midst of modern-day culture, which promotes apocalypse as our most likely future, the words of Black Elk, a Sioux holy man, remind us of the Biblical teaching: 'Where there is no vision, the people perish.' Thus Thomas Berry's proposal of the alternative 'Ecozoic Era', denoting a new age where we live in harmony "with the Earth as our community" feels more constructive and hopeful (c.f. *The Great Work, Our Way into the Future*).

The word 'ecozoic' has its root in the Greek 'zoe', meaning 'life', and in William Blake's mythology, its constituent parts are explored in his vision of *The Four Zoas*. In witnessing the onset of the industrial revolution, Blake saw how 'reason' (what we might now call 'scientific materialism') had come to dominate Western consciousness. Personified as 'Urizen', a patriarchal figure wielding his compass, *The Four Zoas* and *Jerusalem* explore the near annihilation that occurs when Albion ('universal humanity') is subject to urizenic tyranny. The remaining 'zoas' – 'Tharmas' (the body), 'Luvah' (the heart) and 'Urthona' (the imagination), which together constitute the human – are nearly destroyed. Significantly, however, it's the imagination, embodied as Los, the prophet/blacksmith, and Jerusalem, the feminine embodiment of forgiveness, who resist, and finally secure humanity's redemption.

Although Blake's mythology is complex (codified to conceal the dangerously revolutionary implications of his worldview), his work points to the power of the imagination in addressing the ecological crisis we face. Blake's vision of the rebalanced 'four zoas' shows how the imagination can be embodied, connected with the heart and able to get to the root of systemic problems, i.e. radical. In this way, fear and limited thinking can fall away, opening up liminal spaces where our love of freedom can flourish and we can sense the evolving futures we most desire. 'Deep Time, Deep Tissue' and other poems also suggest the labour (personal and collective) required to manifest the Ecozoic Era; as Berry reminds us, this is something "we must will into being".

Intimations at Cae Mabon

The system of naming slate sizes after female nobility was devised by General Hugh Warburton at Penrhyn quarry in 1738. For quarrymen who spoke only Welsh, using these names must have felt alien and an ironic reinforcement of the class divide, but the system became the industry standard, enduring for over two centuries.

I call on the spirit of Owen

In 2012 Frack Off, the campaign organisation leading opposition to fracking in the UK, described 'The Shale Gas Mafia' as: "a powerful group of advisors, donors, non-executive directors and ministers with positions in – or access to – central government. Its vested interests are often centred around companies drilling for unconventional gas. Other figures are lobbyists in government positions whose paymasters include gas companies. This behind-the-scenes influence produces policies as clear as they are brazen: the UK government will support the gas mafia's financial interests no matter what."

Succession, Hampton Court Palace

The term 'wilderness' refers to a place to wander, rather than an uncultivated area of garden. Comprising 18ft high Hornbeam hedges, with interstices planted with Elm, the secluded benches and winding paths made it a place where courtiers could go for privacy.

Sweet Pain

The term 'The Great Turning', popularized by Joanna Macy and David Korten, describes the movement from an industrial-growth society to a life-sustaining one.

Bio tapestry restored by citizens around the world

This piece was inspired by a news report in *The Guardian* on 9.2.13, 'Bayeux tapestry completed by group of Alderney residents'. *Futu* is Guernsey slang, after the French *foutu*, fucked.

About the Author

Helen Moore is an award-winning ecopoet, community artist/ activist and Forest School practitioner based in Somerset, England. Her debut collection, *Hedge Fund – And Other Living Margins* (Shearsman Books, 2012), was described by Alasdair Paterson as being "in the great tradition of visionary politics in British poetry."

Helen has shared conference platforms with modern visionaries such as Joanna Macy, Mathew Fox, Vandana Shiva, Thomas Berry, Patrick Holden and Satish Kumar, and her poems, essays and reviews appear in a wide range of international publications, including *The Wolf, Shearsman Magazine, Long Poem Magazine, Scintilla, Quadrant, Artemis Poetry, Magma, Tears in the Fence, PAN* (*Philosophy, Activism, Nature*), *Ecozon@* (Ecocritical Journal), *Feminist Theology Journal, The Ecologist* (online), *The European Journal of Ecopsychology, Resurgence & The Ecologist, Permaculture Magazine* and *Green Spirit*. She was commissioned as guest editor of the October 2014 issue of *Interalia Magazine*, and chose a theme of Ecocide: Arts, Resistance and Social Change: www.interaliamag.org/issue/ecocide-arts-resistance-and-social-change/

Helen has extensive experience in leading writing workshops within continuing education, schools and community arts programmes, and she particularly enjoys using creative tools to support people's wellbeing outdoors. In 2014 she worked as poet-in-residence for the Bristol Pound, developing people's relationships with their local currency. She is touring 'Green Fire', a collaborative multimedia ecopoetry show with Susan Richardson throughout 2015.

In developing a new artistic sensibility in response to ecocide, Helen explores other genres and art forms too. She has published two children's books about climate change, and in 2011 directed the Web of Life Community Art Project to raise awareness of mass extinction, creating a funeral ceremony in her home-town, Frome. She has also made poetry films in collaboration with film-maker Howard Vause. 'Greenspin', exposing the language of corporate advertising and 'greenwashing', won 3rd prize in the Liberated Words International Poetry Film Festival in 2013. FFI: www.natures-words.co.uk

Acknowledgements

Versions of poems in this collection have previously appeared in the following publications, and I thank the editors: *Shearsman Magazine* – 'Our Daily Bread'; *The Wolf* – 'The Pocket's Circumference', 'Cabinet of Curiosities', 'Succession, Hampton Court Palace'; *Long Poem Magazine* – 'A History of the British Empire in a Single Object', *Scintilla* – 'On Sitting for Christopher Twigg', *Quadrant* – 'Climate Adaptation # 1', 'Egford Brook with Scum', 'Her Feet Speak of the Woman in Heels', 'The Ghosts of Fleas', *Artemis Poetry* – extracts from 'Earth Justice', *Green Spirit* – 'Apple Company, West Country', *Feminist Theology Journal* – 'glory be to Gaia', *The Ecologist* (online), *Her Wings of Glass* (Second Light) – '#Iceclimblive', *The European Journal of Ecopsychology* – 'The Ecopsychologist', *All Our Relations* (a Green Spirit e-book) – 'I Thank my Ancestors', *The Apple anthology* (Nine Arches Press) – 'Aphrodite's Seed'.

'apples are not the only gadgets', '*panem et circenses, 44 BCE – 2012 CE*', 'Kali Exorcism', 'The Flag', Earth Justice', 'Climate Adaptation # 2' and 'Bio tapestry restored by citizens around the world' first appeared with original illustrations in *International Times* (online), www.internationaltimes.it. My thanks to Niall McDevitt, Claire Palmer, David Cooper, Elena Caldera, Nick Victor and Mike Lesser.

'Earth Justice' was awarded 3rd prize in the Second Light Poetry competition 2013, judged by Moniza Alvi, and a recording was previously commissioned by *Resurgence & Ecologist* to mark National Poetry Day 2012. 'glory be to Gaia' was set to music by Guy Wilson and sung by the Web of Life choir at a funeral ceremony for extinct species during the Frome Festival, 2011; it was then sung by a massed choir as part of 'The Great Turning' concert by Prof June Boyce-Tillman at Winchester Cathedral in 2014.

My deepest thanks to Lisa Fannen, Mandy Griffiths and Alex Hart for their support with the evolution of this manuscript. My gratitude also to Niall McDevitt, Maddy Harland, Claire Crowther, John Kinsella, Satish Kumar, Susan Clark, Jay Ramsay, Kevan Manwaring, Olivia Byard, Ian Mowll, Tarisha Finnegan, Rebekah Arthurs, Susan Richardson, Sandeep Parmar, Richard Bright and Nicola Peel for their encouragement and championing of my work. And finally to my students, whose commitment and engagement with learning the craft helps to ensure that poetry remains a vital force in my life.

Books to empower your head, heart and hands

For our full range of titles, to purchase books
and to sign up to our enewsletter see:

www.permanentpublications.co.uk

also available in North America from:

www.chelseagreen.com/permanentpublications